ONCE UPON A DREAM

A Collection Of Verse

Edited By Lynsey Evans

First published in Great Britain in 2024 by:

 YoungWriters Est. 1991

Young Writers
Remus House
Coltsfoot Drive
Peterborough
PE2 9BF
Telephone: 01733 890066
Website: www.youngwriters.co.uk

FOREWORD

Welcome Reader, to a world of dreams.

For Young Writers' latest competition, we asked our writers to dig deep into their imagination and create a poem that paints a picture of what they dream of, whether it's a make-believe world full of wonder or their aspirations for the future.

The result is this collection of fantastic poetic verse that covers a whole host of different topics. Let your mind fly away with the fairies to explore the sweet joy of candy lands, join in with a game of fantasy football, or you may even catch a glimpse of a unicorn or another mythical creature. Beware though, because even dreamland has dark corners, so you may turn a page and walk into a nightmare!

Whereas the majority of our writers chose to stick to a free verse style, others gave themselves the challenge of other techniques such as acrostics and rhyming couplets.

Each piece in this collection shows the writers' dedication and imagination – we truly believe that seeing their work in print gives them a well-deserved boost of pride, and inspires them to keep writing, so we hope to see more of their work in the future!

CONTENTS

Rosa Kelly (8)	65
Joseph Deegan (8)	66
Rory Mulholland (8)	67
Conchúr Savage (8)	68
Carter Madine (8)	69

The Linden Academy Primary School, Luton

Tiana-Bleau Williams (10)	70
Esther Blankson (8)	71
Mydah Khan-Iqbal (10)	72
Elleigh Cauldwell (9)	74
Jewel Amade (9)	75
Bareera Sadiq Akhtar (8)	76
Davin Jesse Paleti (8)	77
Neveah Leith (7)	78
Shabnam Wahid (8)	79
Ania Ahmed (8)	80

Warminster Prep, Warminster

Jonty Cansdale (9)	81
Theo Hall (10)	82
Toby Webber (8)	86
Isabella Thomas (8)	88
Albert Sjo (8)	90
Gray Williams (10)	91
Joshua Coll-Cats (8)	92
Ariana Hare (8)	93

Welton Primary School, Midsomer Norton

Phoebe Handoll (8)	94
Gabriella Monti (8)	95
Elsie Wood (9)	96
William Hall (8)	97
Jake Carroll (9)	98
Amber Dires (9)	99
India Makombe (9)	100
Max Risdale (8)	101
Isaac Dular (8)	102
Rory Cottle (9)	103

Max Button (8)	104
Marley Bugler (9)	105
Lilah Toogood (9)	106
Gesa Surocaj (8)	107
Bradley Adams (8)	108

William De Yaxley CE Academy, Yaxley

Logan Nelder (10)	109
Peggy Minns (10)	110
Ben Woods (10)	112
Marta Bilous (10)	113
Yazmyn Bruce (11)	114
Mary-Jayne Mortlock (10)	115
Daisy Meighan (10)	116
Jessica Bailey (10)	117
Sophie Balaam (8)	118
Harper Devon (7)	119
Violet Hunter (9)	120
Connor Dickson (9)	121
Sonny Rooney (10)	122
Thaian Hoang (11)	123
Skylar Paterson (9)	124
Alicja Skowronska (11)	125
Jack Wright (11)	126
Beau Mills (9)	127
Bradley Holland (10)	128
Isla Barber (9)	129
Isaac Coker (10)	130
Lily Legg (10)	131
Jenson Vellam (11)	132
Emmie Guy (11)	133
Ruby Eaton (11)	134
Madison-Rae Scott (11)	135
Amelia Ayres (11)	136
Summer Ivens (8)	137
Poppy Maxwell (10)	138
Harvey Searle (9)	139
Gabia Datas (9)	140
Teshia Christopher (11)	141
Tyler Johnson (11)	142
Florence Connolly (10)	143
Ellie-Rose Taylor (11)	144

Joshua Pleasance (10)	145	Finley Templeton (10)	188
Noah Giles (10)	146	Aimee Dayman (11)	189
Robin Buckingham (8)	147	Freya Gray (7)	190
Autumn Donachie (8)	148	Teja Gintauskaite (7)	191
Elsie Everett (9)	149	Theo Barton (8)	192
Katie Clarke (8)	150	Leo Cardinal (10)	193
Henry Smith (7)	151		
Jack Nelder (8)	152		
Harvey Renno (10)	153		
Lexi Earl (11)	154		
Ryan Wright (7)	155		
Carter Williams (10)	156		
Lily Forsythe (10)	157		
Aidan Vellam (11)	158		
Dylan Tyler (10)	159		
Mair Powell (9)	160		
Elsie Woods (8)	161		
Henry Ford (10)	162		
Harvey Thain (11)	163		
Jacob Leger (9)	164		
Elizabeth Mallory (10)	165		
Emily Gingell (10)	166		
Lacey Wheeler (11)	167		
Tyler Darby (7)	168		
Jacob Christopher Turnell (10)	169		
Gracie Walton (11)	170		
Poppy Lenton (9)	171		
Oliver Dayman (11)	172		
Freddie Lock (10)	173		
Sophie Toomey (9)	174		
Ethan Everett (11)	175		
Harley Littlechild (10)	176		
Arijus Gintauskas (10)	177		
Victoria Shinyanbola (11)	178		
Emily-Rose Nightingale (7)	179		
Zack Barton (10)	180		
Sienna Devon (10)	181		
Leo Davidson (10)	182		
Jonty Fox (10)	183		
Ellie Renno (9)	184		
Leah Moore (10)	185		
Logan Peeling (9)	186		
Roy Hill (10)	187		

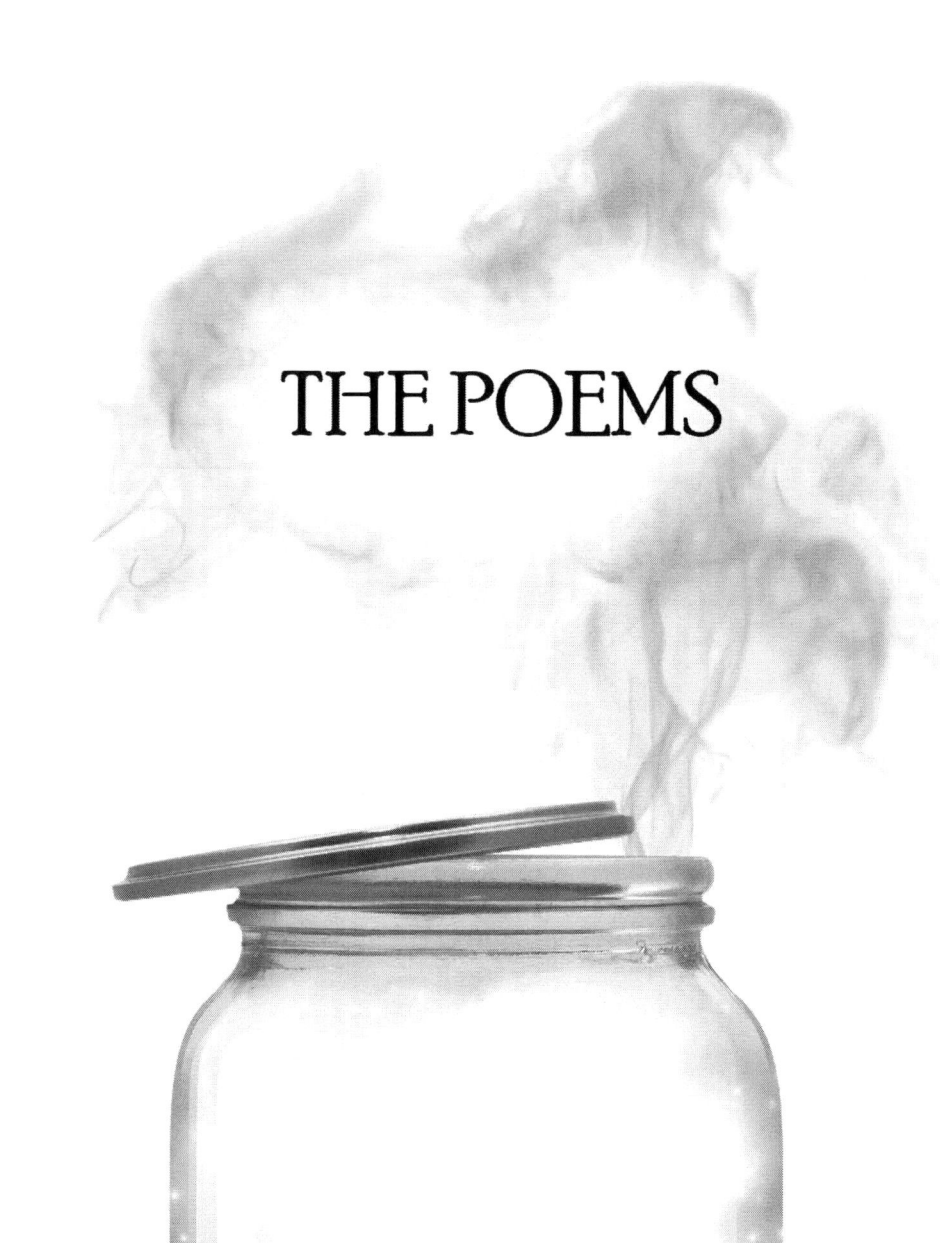

THE POEMS

Future Dreams Of Motocross

There was a gleaming gold trophy and that's what
I wanted,
The sparkling trophy shone so bright,
You didn't even need daylight.

The first race was away to start,
I was hoping I was not going to fart,
So all I need is that gleaming gold trophy,
And if I don't get it I will go away all huffy.

My heart is racing as quick as a flash,
And my brain feels it will burn into ash,
But the best bit is I won the race,
I really put up a very good chase!

The gleaming gold trophy was in my hands,
And I have reached over one hundred thousand fans,
So all I need now is to see my favourite bands,
And I want tasty pancakes cooked in pans.

Now I am the only one that they love,
It's just like being a flying dove,
At the bands they were smacking the drums,
While the whole audience hums.

Brodie Coupland (12)
Aberlour Primary School, Aberlour

1

Football

I always wanted to be a professional football player,
But my coach told me I needed to get taller.
I had a mansion, medals, trophies, and supercars.
I'll be rich and be on a football card, win the World
Cup!
Play for Celtic football team!

The supercars will be really loud and I will have a
private jet.
It will be gold and I will be a football coach,
And buy a plane, a golden plane!
And a football stadium, and a Lego one too.
I will sleep in a golden bed and sofa.

My dream probably won't come true...

Then, I found a portal.
I want to go in but will it delete the world? I don't
know.
I'm going in now...

I went into the portal.
I was in a mansion made from gold.
My dream had come true!

I went to the shop to get football cards.
I opened them... I was on a football card!
My dream had come true!

I had a private jet and supercars.
They were so loud.
I played for Celtic and I won the World Cup!
I had medals and trophies.
I was so happy!
Boom!

I had a supercar!
I paid money for it and I got the car I was happy with.
I had an unlimited prime selection and loads of satisfaction.

Kaleb Shand (10)
Aberlour Primary School, Aberlour

My Perfect Home

A garden filled with pretty pink and yellow tulips,
Wonderful bushes covered with red roses,
Along the stone path, a door of my own,
Painted with my art,
That isn't so dark.
A beautiful archway with gorgeous fairy lights,
And vines at tall heights,
The house is as tiny as a sandcastle,
But that is no hassle.
Inside you'll find a lot of bright colour,
My perfect house is not like any other,
In the living room, the walls are filled with really loud colours,
Through into the kitchen here,
Not a lot of people appear,
Bright blue counters with neon orange walls,
A bowl on the side, with small veg and fruit,
Somewhere near the living room,
I'd have a lovely room, allowing no gloom.
Walls of rainbow and design,
This room won't make you let out a sigh,
Loads of canvasses with tonnes of paint dripping,
Be careful of the paint on the floor,

In case you end up slipping.
My bedroom speaks loudly with colourful walls singing boldly,
My bed is a bit small,
But it is warm and tall,
A bright bookshelf with loads of reading books,
This is my home,
My perfect home.

Saffron Mears (11)
Aberlour Primary School, Aberlour

My Lovely Car

Ever since I was little, I've always wanted a car.
But, sadly, I've never got one, which is rotten
Because the only car I have is made of cotton.

But now is the day I get my new car.
I don't care if it's a Fiat, I really want to see it!
Even an old car will do, as long as there's no dog poo.

I opened the garage door and to my surprise, my thoughts were poor.
The car was luxurious and shimmering in snow.
It drives round and round, never going slow.

It was as fast as light and its might is off the charts!
The exhaust would pop and pop,
Most of the time attracting a distracted cop.

So what, it might cost a lot
What would you rather have, a horse to trot?
Because I wouldn't!

I love my car! I love how it can go over tar without trouble,
And it's so smooth over rubble.

Oh, I love my car.
And you should too.
If you don't, then it's just you.

Logan Duffy (11)
Aberlour Primary School, Aberlour

Nightmare Awoken

I went to bed and couldn't sleep
Then I felt a creep
My wardrobe started to open
Next, I realised a voice had spoken
"I've awoken from my chamber
Now I'm in your farm manger"
The devil has marked his word
I must to listen to what I heard
I'll find his home and start an exorcism
To get rid of this wee bism
In the night, I walked through the forest
Then I watched the stars dance to an angels' chorus
I lay down and fell asleep
As fast as Homer Simpson eating eighty tonnes of meat
I found the devil the next morning
But he was pretty boring
He froze in stone
Then I heard a moan
An angel flew into a rock
Bang, fizzle, pop!
This demon has had an exorcism.
The angel saved me

Now the clouds look happy
But the angel gave me a slappy.

Killin Strachan (10)
Aberlour Primary School, Aberlour

Falling

Trying to sleep in a room nice and dim,
You start to drift off in a bin.
Legs in the air,
Hair on a pear,
Then you start to dream,
You start on the ground and then enter the air.

You're about to jump to go skydiving,
And off you go in the air.
Next thing you know, you're on the go,
Getting lower and lower, you need to pull the cord,
But it turns out you have no cord.

You brought your bag instead of a chute,
You're whizzing down as fast as a bomb.
You hit the ground as you thought,
I landed in a bin?

You look around the little holes,
Then, give your legs a wiggle.
Turns out you are back at home,
With your mum poking you,
"Time for school," she chimes, and you groan.

Martin Pinto Leal (10)
Aberlour Primary School, Aberlour

My Terrifying Teddy Bear

One night I was asleep, but I kept having this
nightmare on repeat,
I was up in my bed when I heard a sound,
I looked around,
What I could see was my favourite teddy, Lee,
I looked closer to see if he was okay,
When suddenly I heard a neigh.
I looked back and then I realised Lee was gone,
My cuddly brown bear with short soft hair,
He was nowhere to be seen.
I got out of bed,
As soon as my foot touched the ground a red light
shone in my eyes,
It gave me a fright,
I went over and then saw Lee,
He had red eyes,
I felt scared and didn't know why he had dripping
blood coming out of his mouth,
It was as red as a tomato,
In his hand, he held a knife.
I ran back to bed and heard a strange sound,
I realised it was all in my head.

Hollie McConnachie (11)
Aberlour Primary School, Aberlour

Creepy Clowns

One creepy, dingy night,
I was awoken by a horrifying laugh,
The wind howling,
And my dad's snoring as loud as waves.
When I looked over to the corner of the room,
There was a glow of red,
Of a red, red nose,
With a killer clown staring at me,
With a gun,
With sharp teeth peering out at me.

I was about to see if he was real,
When something grabbed me down,
And said, "Aren't I funny?"
I snapped back at him,
Saying, "More like a dummy."
He was about to pounce,
When someone started calling my name.
I was horrified,
When I realised, it was my mum calling me to wake up,
That's when I realised it was all a dream,
I was relieved.

Kayla Washborne (10)
Aberlour Primary School, Aberlour

Family Fears

It was a night like any other,
I was saying goodnight to my mother,
"Goodnight," I said,
Then I was off to bed,
Resting my eyes,
I had a crazy dream, to my surprise,
I was in my house, very normal,
Then I saw someone dressed, very formal,
"Evening," he said, in a very posh voice,
"You only have one choice,
Either fight back to your peers,
Or face your family fears!"
"I don't want to fight my fears,"
I said with sweat dripping down my head,
I guess I choose to face my family,
I really, really don't want to fight my peers.

Ruby Geddes (10)
Aberlour Primary School, Aberlour

The Battle Of Gods

It was a dark, gloomy night,
My brother had given me a fright,
He had been fighting a dragon that was as big as a plane,
Its fire looked like a laser,
I had just picked up a taser,
Then I looked for parkour,
To jump on the dragon,
But my brother had been knocked down,
While the moon grinned,
I went to Archie and was sad for his sorrow,
I borrowed the sword he was using,
And killed the deadly dragon,
And survived as a healthy person.
Archie got up and began to laugh,
"I've done it!" he said.
No, give me half of the credit,
I did it as well!

Harvey Spark (10)
Aberlour Primary School, Aberlour

The Great Storm

The cows were mooing,
The sheep were bleating,
As the thunder crackled and popped,
While the river swooshed up to the land,
Flooding the village,
But the farmer did nothing,
He was as calm as can be,
While sipping on his tea.
The rain punched the windows like a boxer,
It was as dark as can be,
I could not see,
It was like a dark cave in the winter,
But the farmer did not care,
His stairs were dancing in the strong wind,
But with the click of the farmer's fingers,
The sky went calm,
And the Northern Lights danced until dawn.

Alastair Macdonald (11)
Aberlour Primary School, Aberlour

My Lorry Horror

I was awoken with a bang; it was just a blunder,
I wondered what it was, but then I saw the road,
All there was were trees galore and the sprinkling of
the moon,
With a zoom, a car whizzed past, I was still not fully
awake,
Then I saw a bright light; it was a trailer,
I was in shock, with a flash it was on, and I was gone,
But then he arrived; he was as tall as a tree,
I was sure he would get me,
I stepped on the gas and drove, but then a crash,
I awoke, I was shaking, wondering what had happened,
But I just shrugged it off and went to bed.

James Hanton (11)
Aberlour Primary School, Aberlour

My F1 Dream To Win A Grand Prix

Vroom!
The kart engines stated,
The large exhaust roared and the race was swerving through the positions,
All was well until, *bang!*
It was my engine,
It had blown,
I pulled into the side in rage slamming on my steering wheel,
I thought my dream was over until a man approached me,
He invited me to drive for MP Motorsport,
My dream might not be over,
I had my first race on a track in the middle of Austria,
I started eighth,
Broom, broom!

Harry Younie (11)
Aberlour Primary School, Aberlour

Pirate Adventure!

In my dreams one special night,
I saw a pirate fight!
A giant purple Kraken,
With tentacles bigger than buses,
And scaly skin just like a snake!
It clung to the ship with all its might,
And it gave us all quite a fright,
As the boat splashed side to side,
Everything was so loud!
Bang, splosh, bang!
Then the Kraken let go,
And we all danced and pranced,
And even the ship was happy!
But then suddenly I woke up in my bed!

Nikola Carvalho (10)
Aberlour Primary School, Aberlour

My Dream About Me At A West Ham Match

My dream was me at the London Stadium, in 2022,
Wonderful West Ham vs lovely Liverpool,
When Pablo Fornals scores an excellent goal
From the corner spot,
Then Firmino scored for Liverpool,
But after that, Fornals made another incredible goal,
Then Bowen scored for West Ham as well,
We were leading 3-1,
Until Origi came on and did a brilliant goal,
For luxury Liverpool,
To end the match 3-2,
West Ham won
And Liverpool lost.

Finlay Langley (11)
Aberlour Primary School, Aberlour

Monsters

Monsters are scary,
Monsters are hairy,
Monsters are tall.
Monsters are low,
And they follow me everywhere I go.

Some have two eyes,
Some have three eyes,
Some have five eyes,
Some have six,
Some smell good, not like mud,
Some are smelly, just like wellies.

Until one follows me,
"I need to be fed," it said,
But then I wake up,
And I'm home in my bed.

Eleanor Akakpo (10)
Calverley Parkside Primary School, Calverley

Lots Of Spiders

Spiders, spiders, in my hair,
Spiders, spiders, everywhere,
Spiders, spiders, help me, please!
Spiders, spiders, trapped with these,
Spiders, big, spiders small,
Spiders short, spiders tall,
Spiders scary,
Spiders mean,
Spiders creeping over me,
Wake up, it's okay, you can do it anyway!
No need to shout,
No need to scream,
All of that was just a dream!

Skye Brennan (10)
Calverley Parkside Primary School, Calverley

Me And My PC!

What can I see, me and my PC,
Monitor, headset, speakers, and me.
Fortnite, FIFA, Mario and Minecraft,
Just me and my PC.
I can only see me and my PC,
Resting, rocking on my gaming chair, just me.
No one to stop me as I race through records,
Just on my PC.
No wonder or wish is a greater gift,
To dream about me and my perfect PC!

Isaac Dixon (10)
Calverley Parkside Primary School, Calverley

Deep Water

When I'm sleeping, I see my friend, Josh,
We embark on an adventure,
The middle of the lake is as dark as a pit,
But don't worry, keep reading, stick with it!
The moon came out and shone as bright as a star,
We were horrified as roaring noises came from afar,
Suddenly, we found ourselves on top of a beast,
Who I think wanted to make us his tasty feast!
As his razor teeth came toward me,
I knew my life was coming to an end,
The sea beast's eyes closed,
His bright, orange, piercing eyes,
He sprinted ahead to our boat,
In the middle of the deep, dark lake,
We saw our life shine before us,
Is this really the end?
The beast was angry at the sight
Of me and my friend, Josh,
As the fear took over, we turned around and ran
Toward the light.

Alexander Oles (10)
St Charles RC Primary School, Swinton

The Dream

T he field was luscious as can be, me sitting on a blanket what a dream this could be,

H igh up in the blue sky roared, with calming colours I love it, give me some more,

E very second I would see new white, black, and orange-furred rabbits, please say this is not a dream.

D reaming is fun I wish it was real, and behind me was a flabbergasting surprise. I just can't believe it was my family now my eyes are in streams,

R ight, left is paradise I thought but then giraffes were running on paths, it was like a stampede.

"E ating is fun too," I said, pushing my luck and luck that hundreds of my favourite foods popped out and I was hungry with no doubt about it.

A fter this, it was the best of all. My mum left for twenty minutes (you may be thinking how is this good, well read on and find out). In the meantime, I played with my younger siblings, tig to be exact, and when she returned she had the biggest smile in the world and she told me... all her problems with her heart were gone!

M y dream was so famous I sold it for millions but that was a dream too...

That is the end of...
The Dream.

Jon-Paul Flynn (10)
St Charles RC Primary School, Swinton

One Piece

In my dreams, I join a pirate crew,
Who have strange names like Billy the Piper Poo,
They dress me in a pirate costume,
And teach me how to scrub the decks,
Big silver necklaces hang from their old dirty necks,
The captain says I'm not good enough,
I'll show him Mr Tough,
I get the secret gum-gum fruit,
Whilst I'm shining the captain's boots,
I feel scared as I've taken loot,
Scrubbing the deck,
I hear the birds peck,
I go to eat my hungry feast,
As the ship sails northeast,
The captain stops me but he does it too soon,
My arm stretched like a balloon,
The captain tells me my body turns to rubber,
As I've lost my ability to swim forever,
I start blinking a lot and believe,
I'm in my bed, not sailing at sea.

Boris Nweyadye (9)
St Charles RC Primary School, Swinton

Animals Of The World

I close my eyes, ready for bed,
And a bunch of animals are going through my head.
I see a monkey that climbs,
Like Tarzan swinging from the vines.
I notice a horse, going, "Neigh!"
That's all he says throughout the day.
I notice a cat wearing a funny top hat.
He loved that top hat, but he got tired, so he sat.
There was a sea with a whale.
I found that all when I took a boat and set sail.
I looked around and saw a dark-hearted dragon, breathing fire
And to kill was his only desire.
Jumping around was a bunny.
The other animals said, "He only jumps like that when it's sunny!"
All these animals, you have met,
Are soon to be my pet.
I hope the animals make me feel joyful and free,
I want them to do that for eternity.

Callum Malley (9)
St Charles RC Primary School, Swinton

The Magical Journey Of Two Brothers

I fell out of the sky onto my broom,
As I whizzed through the air I cast a spell,
I wondered how many people could tell.
Maybe there are other wizards around,
I'd like to see if any are found.
My hair was blowing as I cast my spell,
As I broke through a wall there was a terrible smell.
I go to Platform Nine and Three Quarters to get
my train,
I've done it before, I'll do it again.
Off to the wizardly world, I go,
First I must get my brother,
He is notoriously slow.
He wears the sorting hat,
Gryffindor has been decided and that is that.
We go around our magical school together,
Thinking this is now a great pleasure.
At last in our favourite place,
I feel excited we're together, at last in this dream.

Henry Eaton (9)
St Charles RC Primary School, Swinton

The One Piece

In my dream, I'm swinging in a hammock
Angry faces were staring down at me
As I wore a worried face
Cannons firing very loudly
People shouting all around me
To my shock and surprise
I discovered my new power
I have the power to control darkness
I can strike the most powerful ships
At the speed of light
Tentacles surround me
The ship had haunted powers
Controlling the tentacle as they attacked the other ship
My powers grew stronger
Energy rushed through my body
Electrifying power rushed through my veins
Crash!
I struck the ship
Terrifying tentacles started to disappear
My eyes started to flicker
The dream was so clear
I hope my powers weren't fake.

Adam Glowienkowski (10)
St Charles RC Primary School, Swinton

31 Nights In The Middle Of Nowhere

In the middle of nowhere,
where the light flickers so I can see,
an empty room stands before me.

All of a sudden, I start to sweat...
When I breathe, I'm breathing fire.
I open the window to see
the moon shining brightly on me.

Slowly, the camouflaged door opens wide.
I am feeling nervous, what a fright!
Before my eyes, zombies charged at me.
As fast as Usain Bolt, my body wakes
with a bolt of lightning.

The door encloses opens, which is a wall.
As I ran so fast, I took a fall.
A deep, dark forest surrounded me.
Then I wondered, would somebody find me
in this mysterious place?

Alfie Kennedy (9)
St Charles RC Primary School, Swinton

The Bee Curse

A bee was flying in my room,
All I could hear was *zoom! Zoom! Zoom!*
I opened my window to let it out,
But the next minute I gave a shout!
The bee had stung me,
I felt so small,
Suddenly, I was buzzing up a wall,
The bee curse had infected me,
I felt like a honey bee,
I flew through the window,
And found a sleeping man,
And all of a sudden, I had a cunning plan,
I lunged at him and jabbed him with my sting,
I noticed my wing was human again,
There was an almighty scream,
It was just a dream.

Joseph Hayes (10)
St Charles RC Primary School, Swinton

Dragon Fight

Me and my friend climbed the enormous rocky
mountain,
To kill the evil fire-breathing dragon.
When we got to the top,
It was quiet, too quiet.
The evil dragon flew down from the top of the
mountain, lighting up the sky with flames,
The battle began.
The knights' swords flew and then slashed,
The archer's arrow soared through the sky,
We used our fireball spell.
Then, the evil dragon flew off into the distance,
I woke up; when my mum turned on the light.

Noah Lancaster (10)
St Charles RC Primary School, Swinton

Shapeshifter

S hapeshifters watching you
H earing you, watching you
A ppearing out of nowhere
P eering through the darkness
E erie and suspicious.
S uspicious people watching and listening
H iding where they can't be found
I nside your room, hiding from you
F eeling you, listening to your dreams
T hey're in your bedroom
E ntering and exiting through the window
R emembering you are there.

Sebastian Allan (10)
St Charles RC Primary School, Swinton

Nigel, The Flying Horse

Flying high on Nigel the horse,
I feel so happy and surprised,
The wind blowing through my hair,
I don't have a single care,
Flying over people and buildings tall,
My family and friends wouldn't believe it at all,
Jumping and flipping me over and over,
The bright blue sky fills me with joy,
I suddenly wake and find myself hugging,
Nigel the flying horse toy,
The toy was cuddly, but no wings could be seen,
Oh no, was this really just a dream?

Rose Hall (10)
St Charles RC Primary School, Swinton

Freedom

When I was young I would imagine I could fly,
I would go anywhere I could fly so high,
I could fly to space and look at the shining stars,
Seeing all of the planets made me feel so calm,
I would fly with the birds and my friends,
And all the enjoyment would never end,
I could travel the world and be so free,
There were so many beautiful sights I could see,
I met so many people and no one was mean,
But then sadly I woke up and it was all a dream.

Annie Haywood (10)
St Charles RC Primary School, Swinton

Game Day

I always like to run.
It's normally really fun!
But this is a race,
Where you have to keep the pace.
With every step I take,
It feels like my heart is about to break!
All of a sudden, I fall.
All I can hear is a faint call.
On the floor, I feel very sore.
All I needed to do was win.
All my scholarship dreams are in the bin!

One by one, they pass the finish line!
How dare they take what is mine?

Matylda Afuwape (9)
St Charles RC Primary School, Swinton

Spiders Made Me Crash

Nothing prepared me for this shock,
My arms are wriggling; my head is locked.
There is nothing to do,
There are some sort of spiders in my hair,
It made me think that I was in a dare.

My family is shocked that I am there,
My mum is screaming; my dad is nowhere.
My head is itching; I fell to the ground with a big crash,
This birthday party is the worst,
I felt so angry, I am going to burst.
Spiders invading my party,
It made me want to run away.

Emily Curry (9)
St Charles RC Primary School, Swinton

A Cat Named Stanly

In my dreams every night,
I go to school and have a fright,
When I come home I go up the stairs,
But no hope is there,
My mum shouts me down,
So I go,
And there to my surprise,
A cute kitten as white as snow,
I prance and dance,
His name is Stanly,
Like someone in my family,
I calm him down,
As he gave a sad frown,
Mum shouts, "Breakfast!"
And it was all a dream.

Charlotte Condron (9)
St Charles RC Primary School, Swinton

Gamer

I dream of being a famous gamer,
TikTok, YouTube, and all of my favourites.
People follow me from all over the world.
One million subscribers I've heard,
Happiness is playing with my friends,
It's so sad when a game has to end,
One day I will have my own YouTube channel,
I can't wait until that day comes,
Playing and gaming just like I do,
Until all that effort does all it needs to do.

Seb Jones (10)
St Charles RC Primary School, Swinton

Pumpkin Pie

In my dreams I see
A dragon's eye,
Eating my delicious pumpkin pie,
In the sun,
I drink my Capri Sun,
I was having so much fun,
In the clouds,
I hear a sound,
It made me stutter,
Where's the butter?
It was the last ingredient
To make my famous pumpkin pie,
I could maybe try,
I started to cry,
And realised,
Thank goodness,
It is just a dream.

Libby Boyd (10)
St Charles RC Primary School, Swinton

The Dancer

In my dreams,
I love to dance,
Turning and jumping,
Now I prance,
My leg kicks high,
On the ballet bar,
My teachers think,
I'm a natural star.
Soaring through the air,
With glitter in my hair,
Going to Hollywood,
Catching a plane and a train,
All my hard work,
Dedicated to this day,
Lying on my bed,
All I can say,
Is thank you for today.

Lilly-Rose Kwiatek (9)
St Charles RC Primary School, Swinton

Fluffy, Snuggly Grey Bunny

I dreamt I could fly,
Me and my bunny flying high in the sky,
I took her hand as we drifted along,
I got a tingly feeling inside;
Has happiness arrived?
We flew through clouds as fluffy as candyfloss,
We jumped into creamy chocolate.
The sky turned rainbow red,
Is this real or am I home, tucked up in bed?
Such a magical feeling,
Will I ever stop dreaming?

Elizabeth Whisker (10)
St Charles RC Primary School, Swinton

Top Corner

In my dreams, every night,
I scored the most amazing bicycle kick,
Jumping so high, like Garnacho,
The crowd screamed as I did a knee slide,
In the locker room, watching the replay,
I lift the Premier League trophy into the sky,
As I looked around, I saw my dad,
He laughed and cheered,
Along with the crowd,
I know my dad is so proud.

Ralph Lingard (9)
St Charles RC Primary School, Swinton

Football

F irst match I get nervous,
O ut on the pitch I see my opponent,
O h no, the crowd roared,
T ension built as the match started,
B ooing and cheering is all I could hear,
A pproaching the goal I see my target,
L ouder and louder the crowd become,
L eaping for joy I score my first goal.

Johnny Lee (9)
St Charles RC Primary School, Swinton

A Surprise!

I was surprised with a kitten,
That was as cute as a mitten,
It pranced and leaped,
Would it ever sleep?
I was overcome with joy,
Was it a girl or a boy?
A boy, I was told,
To keep warm in the cold,
He was so cute,
I nearly dressed him in a suit,
Soon I was awake,
Realising it was a dream and it was all fake.

Emma Davies (9)
St Charles RC Primary School, Swinton

Clowns

Walking back from a fair
I turned around to see a clown with an ominous stare
I ran as fast as I could
My heart was beating. What a blast!
Inside the safety of my house
I hid in the basement with Winnie the mouse
Bang! Bang! Bang!
He was inside
I was petrified
Suddenly Mum shouted, "Breakfast!"

Finn Cahill (9)
St Charles RC Primary School, Swinton

Murder Mystery: Nightmare

In my dreams, pitch-black darkness
Makes me feel scared.
I am alone in my flat.

My cute dog, Sammy, has my back.
He barked so loud, his ears cracked!
I drifted back to sleep.

But later on, I was disturbed.
The door clicked...
When they came in, I screamed!
Thank goodness it was just a dream!

Ben Maly (10)
St Charles RC Primary School, Swinton

The Adventures Of James And Rory

I wake up from a sleepover with Rory
The sun shines very brightly in my bedroom
Suddenly I see a flash of light
A mysterious machine appears in the corner
I quickly wake Rory
A mysterious voice came out of the machine saying
"Come in"
We step in and suddenly, *snap!*
The door closes, and all we see is a shiny light saying
'2074'
And *whoosh, creeak!*
It was amazing
A high-tech city awaits us
Firstly we ate some cheeseburgers with chips
It was all great
Until we bumped into one of the King's guards
"Aliens!" the guard shouted
A herd of guards came. "Get them!"
"Argghh!"

James Magee (8)
St Patrick's Primary School, Saul

Dinosaur World

I woke up and felt quite small,
I felt ill and sick,
I felt like a snail climbing over me.
I woke up under a hill,
I felt dizzy, like twisting around,
I realised I was in a dinosaur world!

There was no one around me so far,
Suddenly, I heard a loud noise.
I don't hear it anymore. I felt great.
It was really hot.
I saw a T-rex, I got scared,
I ran away; my heart was pounding,
I had to hide.

I hid in a tight space,
The dinosaur ran past me.
There was another dinosaur,
They fought, and one bled.
The other one was bleeding,
I ran away and hid myself.
Someone was coming,
They shot the dinosaurs,
I woke up screaming!

Cormac Hanna (8)
St Patrick's Primary School, Saul

My Final

I was with my team,
Van Dijk, Alisson, Salah, Jota,
My rivals and my fans,
Kick off!
I am nervous,
They scored 1-0,
Then again, 2-0,
Another, 3-0,
The referee blows his whistle,
It's half-time,
Second half,
Van Dijk, 1-3,
Then 2-3,
We score!
3-3,
My team are celebrating with the fans,
Last minute Salah crossed to me in the box,
I'm about to score!
Tackle!
Penalty, yellow card,
But he checked VAR,
Red card!

I step up,
I score,
Goal!
And then we lifted the trophy,
And we are roaring like lions!

Jenson Smyth (8)
St Patrick's Primary School, Saul

The Underwater Dream

Once upon a time, I had a dream,
I ended up in the sea,
But not any type of sea,
It was a magical type of sea,
The water was as smooth as glass,
The coral was like emerald green,
And the fish were like rainbows,
Suddenly, I turned into a mermaid,
From a big splash of water,
I had one pet and it was my dolphin,
My home was a beautiful pink shell,
The school was near a shimmering rock,
The best bit was the diamond cave,
There was a park made out of coral reef,
And it is red, orange, yellow, green, blue and pink,
I don't want this magical world to end.

Helenka Tylkowski (8)
St Patrick's Primary School, Saul

The Time Machine

In the forest there is a time machine
On Sunday I see it out of the corner of my eye
Then I go over to it, but it is broken!
I try to fix it, but I can't because it is as old as time
But, with a simple kick
It takes me back in time, to the Dinosaur Age
Giant, scary dinosaurs are showing their teeth
They start to roar. It scares me!
Then they chase me over to a cave
I hide inside the cave, but then I see
A caveman! I try to hide, but he finds me
Luckily he is nice. We become friends.
Me and the caveman find a fossil
When I wake up, I'm still holding it!

Louis Smyth (7)
St Patrick's Primary School, Saul

White Hart Lane

The first of the season in White Hart Lane.
I'm nervous...
I walk out of the tunnel.
The crowd is cheering, "Come on you Spurs!"

The drums banging, the crowd cheering
as loud as possible.

The match starts, 0-0 at half-time.
2nd half starts, they score in the 60th minute!
The Spurs crowd is starting to get louder.

I get a free kick outside the box.
I shoot and score!
The Spurs crowd is going mental!

I got man of the match!
I was proud of myself!

Darragh McGoran (8)
St Patrick's Primary School, Saul

Chocolate Heaven

A normal day
Dozing with Cleo my cat
Suddenly, we're teleported to Willy Wonka's factory
We're all amazed, we can't believe our eyes
Everything is edible, even the grass
Wonka appeared and he was as cross as a weasel
Lollipop trees, cotton candy bushes
All gone in our tummies
We felt quite queasy
Also quite bad
His dreams were crushed
It was very sad
I touched the portal
Thankfully, we were back home
I woke up hungry.

Callum Denvir (8)
St Patrick's Primary School, Saul

My Underwater Adventure

I was exhausted after swimming
I fell into a deep sleep
I woke up underwater!
With Maria next to me, we didn't know what happened
The water was as cold as ice!
I saw a castle in the distance
When we got there, I saw the king of the sea!
He was upset because someone stole the heart of
the sea
I made it my mission to find it!
Two weeks later I found the heart of the sea!
I got rewarded by being turned into a mermaid!
I love being a mermaid.

Mila Quinn (8)
St Patrick's Primary School, Saul

Untitled

My dad and I were trapped in a haunted house
with a clown and dragons
It was scary
And we were in the basement when my dad found
a light
Haunted house
Creepy and dark
The haunted house stood still
My dad and I were trapped there
Clowns and dragons came out
I screamed
The clown heard it
"Who is there?" he shouted
Then my dad found a light
It was all fine in the basement.

Harry McMullan (8)
St Patrick's Primary School, Saul

My Little Kitty Cat

One sunny day,
my cat, Sumo, was on the grass
playing with his toy mouse.

Rio, my other cat,
jumped and frightened him!
He frightened me too!

I turned into a cat.
I'm black and white.

I had the best day ever
playing with my cat on the
big bales of hay in the field.

Then, my best friend, Alisha,
came with some cotton candy
and then I turned back to me.

Megan Mullan (8)
St Patrick's Primary School, Saul

The Royal Makeover

Just a normal day,
I heard a knock on the door,
I answered the door,
The next thing you know,
It is the royal Queen at the door,
I was so excited, I was in shock,
The Queen asked if she could have a makeover,
And she said yes,
So I got to it,
I got my bits and bobs,
I got started,
When I was finished,
The Queen loved it,
She said thank you,
In a poof, she was gone.

Isabelle Farrell (8)
St Patrick's Primary School, Saul

Ella The Good Dragon

I'm Ella the dragon,
I protect big, small, and even tiny,
But mostly the magical forest,
But when night strikes it gets badder and badder,
And the monsters come out!
There it gets scary,
Then the big bad wolf comes out,
All the little creatures run away,
By the big bad wolf,
But nobody could stop him,
Until my dog comes,
To save the day!

Elise Carr (7)
St Patrick's Primary School, Saul

The Winning Goal

Anfield is my dream
I have always wanted to play there
The smell of the grass
The roar of the crowd
My heart was pounding
The other team scored
I started to get worried
The match was nearly over
But then I got tackled in the box
I got a penalty...
I scored!
I did it!
I saved the day,
The winning goal was mine.

Tadhg Bohill (7)
St Patrick's Primary School, Saul

Dragon Doom

I was playing with Elise,
I felt heat across my shoulder.
Could it be dragon breath?
I was terrified, I looked around.
The house was empty, everyone was gone.
I looked and what a sight!
I saw dragons flying in circles,
Making dark shadows past my house.
Elise screamed and I fainted.
Then I woke from a terrible dream!

Fionn Magee (7)
St Patrick's Primary School, Saul

I Love Liverpool

It is my dream to go to Anfield.
One night I dreamt I played in Anfield,
I was so happy.
The other team scored,
It was nearly the end of the match.
I was on goal and I got tackled.
I got a free kick and I shot and I scored
And I scored again.
I got man of the match,
I was so happy!
Then I woke up!

Conor Magee (8)
St Patrick's Primary School, Saul

My Adventure In The Forest

In the forest, I hear birds sing.
I went down to the river and collected some flowers for the new day.
I gave my flowers to all of the fairies.
I then stepped on a rock and fell down underground,
My horse knew there was something wrong,
I saw gold,
I went back up,
My horse was there,
I gave her a big hug!

Maria Byrne (8)
St Patrick's Primary School, Saul

Dancing With The Pop Stars

Day after day,
I asked to join the nice dance class,
Certainly they like to prance!
Every time I ask, they say no
Instead one day they said "Yes!"
I was bubbling with excitement
And I couldn't believe it!
Isabelle, Emma, and Alisha
Were there dancing with the pop stars too!

Rosa Kelly (8)
St Patrick's Primary School, Saul

My Anfield Adventure

Excitement is rising,
New players to play and I'm going to Anfield today,
I realise that I'm sitting beside Robbie Fowler!
After the game, I got his signature,
It was amazing,
I had a tour of the stadium,
Mo Salah asks me to play,
I can't believe it,
My dream has come true!

Joseph Deegan (8)
St Patrick's Primary School, Saul

My Robot House

I was in my home and I saw a magic drone,
I followed it and saw the levers,
I flicked a lever,
And a robot as big as can be appeared,
Then it jumped into space,
Bringing me too!
"Help us!" we shouted,
The robot fuelled up and took us home,
I was so happy to be home.

Rory Mulholland (8)
St Patrick's Primary School, Saul

The Big Bonfire

It was a lovely night,
It was a clear sky,
Me, my dad and friends went to gather stuff up,
It was 8.30,
We stacked the twigs and tyres,
Then it was 8.50,
And some people started to arrive,
We lit it,
The flames licked the sky,
It was amazing!

Conchúr Savage (8)
St Patrick's Primary School, Saul

My Winter Wonderland

I had a dream,
I was in a winter wonderland,
It was ice cold,
Me, Harry, Finn and Cormac,
Were shivering like mad,
There were polar bears and penguins,
Sliding down a snow hill,
We found an igloo to stay in.

Carter Madine (8)
St Patrick's Primary School, Saul

The Spirits Of The House

Down inside that eerie haunted house,
Lies the spirit of the mysterious, manipulative mouse.
His disappearance was quite unlike anything else,
No trace of the criminal.
All we know is that his clothes are oversized,
Long, and a dusty kind of white.
Some say his last words were my name,
But I think they are just being lame.
When I look out my window, my neighbour I see
Looking like he's sent that mouse to come for me.
One rainy night a knock gave me a fright,
I walk down the stairs. *Creak, creak.*
But it seems like someone's watching me,
I turn around to see the deep, dark night.
And I see a silhouette, vast and wide,
Like when a tree reflects the light
Being scared, I ran back to bed as fast as my feet could
carry me,
I turn on the light, but I feel like someone is lurking
from that night.

Tiana-Bleau Williams (10)
The Linden Academy Primary School, Luton

A Spectacular Train Journey

Clickety-clack goes the train on the track.
How far did we go? How far did we go?
Nobody ever knew.

The excitement is building up inside of me,
As we are approaching our destination.
I am sitting around the table,
Next to my friend Chloe and my brothers,
Mum is sitting next to us on the opposite table.

When I look out of the window,
I see fluffy, white sheep that look like clouds...
Green, green grass on the green, green fields.

The train driver announces,
"We have arrived at Luton Station."
We hurry to get to the doors,
I press the green button,
The doors slide open like the hungry jaws of a lion.

Esther Blankson (8)
The Linden Academy Primary School, Luton

Next Time I'm Staying In Bed

My alarm goes off,
The sky is still dark and the birds are tweeting,
I get out of bed and open my blinds,
Open my window and go downstairs,
The house is silent,
The rooms are vacant,
I shout for my parents,
There's no reply,
It was so silent,
I could hear a feather hit the floor,
As I was about to call for my parents again,
I heard a sudden thud from the basement,
Reluctantly I went to investigate,
My heart was thumping,
I felt a shiver go down my spine,
I went down the basement stairs,
I opened the wooden door and scanned around,
My ears started ringing like a bell at the sight,
Of a sickening bright light,
I ran upstairs,
I went to my bedroom,
I opened my door,
And hid in my bed,

Never again,
Next time I'm staying in bed.

Mydah Khan-Iqbal (10)
The Linden Academy Primary School, Luton

Midnight

Nightmares come and haunt your dreams,
They say it's not real, that's not how it seems,
They come and give you a fright,
There's no point trying to fight,
They will just come back and haunt your dreams,
You may be curious how they happen,
Boy, you don't want to know they're so vicious,
Sometimes they're scary,
Sometimes they're eerie and gloomy,
Once I had a nightmare, man it was spooky!
There were blood-curdling noises,
It was very petrifying,
When the floors tremble,
Someone's lurking in the dark,
You can hear footsteps like crazy,
They give me goosebumps!

Elleigh Cauldwell (9)
The Linden Academy Primary School, Luton

Ancient Curious Visions

Dark eerie nights,
Something dark comes to your mind,
Seeing gnarly, surprised visions,
Your head thinks of therapy sessions,
An ancient, curious sound comes to mind,
A true spirit of visions to find,
In visions, enchanted, beastly, fearsome pain,
Scanning the unexpected, weird veins,
Suddenly, a tingling sound calls us as cold as ice,
Visions I see, monstrous, unpleasant sounds, like mice,
Nightmares freshly sharpened with fire,
Visions from past to future,
Some are alarming torture,
Deep, beep, sea, tea,
It could be about anything.

Jewel Amade (9)
The Linden Academy Primary School, Luton

A Day With A Fairy

We walked among the flowers
Under the starry night
We laughed and sang for hours
Feeling happy and bright
Then we saw a fairy
Sparkling in the air
She was lovely and pretty
We couldn't help but stare
She smiled and waved at us
And invited us to play
We joined her and had a magical day
We danced and played together
Until we were tired
We thanked her for the adventure
And then we moved along
We will never forget that night
When we saw a fairy in the sky.

Bareera Sadiq Akhtar (8)
The Linden Academy Primary School, Luton

The Future

I always dream about what I'll become in the future
Sometimes I dream that I'll become a skydiver
Or a professional footballer
Or even a famous celebrity
I never dream of it being bad
I always dream of it being good
Maybe once in a blue moon
I dream of something bad
But it's mostly always good
Once I dreamt I was in a land of dreams
In the morning after that dream
I felt special, useful and important.

Davin Jesse Paleti (8)
The Linden Academy Primary School, Luton

The Talent Show

Once upon a time,
there lived a girl named Heaven.

I got invited to Britain's Got Talent.
I even invited my friend to go with me.
I felt very happy!

I was surprised when they called my name
as I know how to sing.
After I sang, they called my friend.

My friend performed perfectly
and I won Britain's Got Talent.

Neveah Leith (7)
The Linden Academy Primary School, Luton

Dance As You Wish

Let's set the standards as high as the sky
With our dance floor moving harder and faster.

Let's party on the dance floor
Until we can hear laughter everywhere.

Without a doubt in the world,
Dance as if it was our last chance.

I see nothing except me dancing in front of a mirror
Let the happiness flow within the music.

Shabnam Wahid (8)
The Linden Academy Primary School, Luton

The Angel's Story

Within the wind,
Shone an angel,
A kind angel,
A majestic angel,
White, grand and powerful,
There it stood with its feather-filled wings,
Ready to fly across the blue sky.
Within the wind,
There it flew with guards and friends,
The majestic, white, kind angels,
Smiled at me as I slept soundly,
As I was dreaming.

Ania Ahmed (8)
The Linden Academy Primary School, Luton

Out Of Space Flying

In my dreams I fly to space,
I have to say it's really ace,
When I'm there, I make a friend,
We fight to avoid a sticky end.

We see an astronaut diving from planet to planet,
Like some kind of sea creature or space gannet,
His spaceship, he left all alone,
We jumped aboard to take us home.

George Washington jumped on the bow,
With the astronaut, he had a row,
He'd been stung by a big space bee,
So we took him back to old DC.

But halfway through, we broke down,
Thanks to a revolting little clown,
And then we went into a black hole,
And I woke up to see I still had my soul!

Jonty Cansdale (9)
Warminster Prep, Warminster

Dino Disco

I brush my teeth, put my PJ's on,
Snuggle in bed with all lights gone,
Can't wait to be dreaming,
Definitely not scheming,
My eyelids begin to droop,
My imagination goes loop the loop,
Suddenly in the distance I can see,
A hazelnut door as welcoming as can be,
What could be behind that door?
A nasty little horror scene?
Something that will make me scream?
Or could it be a unicorn with snow-white fur and
a sparkling horn?
I ponder there for a while,
Then open the door with a smile,
Before my eyes is a magical land,
With tropical trees and glistening sand,
Turquoise sky and a golden sun,
Puffy white clouds, oh what fun!
Then a shadow creeps across the sky,
A flying spotty dinosaur, my oh my,
It drifts through the diamond air,
Like it doesn't have a care,

It is joined by a purple octopus,
All majestic and quite pompous,
Wiggling its tentacles to and fro,
I wonder which way it's going to go,
Suddenly there is a bubbling sound,
And out from the lake comes something shaking the ground,
A bright stripe pink and orange tyrannosaurus rex,
What on earth is going to happen next?
A massive fluffy yellow spine,
Glides along the watery brine,
Diving down below the depths,
It pops back up, I hold my breath,
Then I notice something strange about this creature,
It has rather chicken-like features,
Feathery wings and an orange beak,
This monster is truly quite unique,
I am just admiring him when I see
Something in the distance, what can it be?
Flashing lights and a disco ball,
The disco ball was definitely not small,
Coming from a mountainous rock.
The next thing that happens gives me a frightful shock,
All the creatures stopped and stared,
It was as though they were all prepared,

The beasts rush towards the mountain range,
Then I spy something else strange,
Other creatures join the parade,
It made me feel quite afraid,
I followed them at a steady jog,
And I am joined by a see-through frog,
"Where are they going?" I asked the amphibian.
"Why, they're going to the mountain of oblivion,"
He croaks in reply and then hops away,
I travel on, will it be okay?
I trek along past rivers and trees,
I reach the foot of the mountain with ease,
Stopping there to take a break,
I hear music that makes the ground shake,
As I climb the mountain the beats get louder,
Under my feet lies the snowy powder,
As I reach the top I look straight down,
My mouth drops open, I start to frown,
Then a smile spreads across my face,
I can't believe this amazing place,
A kaleidoscope of colours, flashing lights,
Creaturs dancing, some in flight,
Hipping, hopping, bipping and bopping,
Raving and waving, never stopping,
The octopus that I saw before,

Is waving his tentacles all over the floor,
The giant chicken, break dancing everywhere,
Flapping his feathers, he just doesn't care,
They spy me watching and beckon me over,
I feel as lucky as a four-leaf clover,
I strut my stuff and wiggle about,
Looking around I pose and pout,
I close my eyes and swing and sway,
But the music retreats further away,
Why is it stopping, has it lost its charm?
What's that I hear, not my alarm,
I don't want to wake up, it isn't right,
My eyelids flicker in the morning light,
I open my eyes to see my boring ceiling,
Giving me such a downward feeling,
I am in my home in San Fransisco,
And no longer at the Dino Disco!

Theo Hall (10)
Warminster Prep, Warminster

Once Upon A Dream

Once upon a dream, I went into a dark wood,
I saw someone with a crooked hood,
I was not sure who it was.
Could it be the Wizard of Oz?

Slowly, I went up to the man.
Suddenly, *bang!*
I was terrified, I was not sure what to do!

I ran so fast, I lost my shoe!
I hopped and skipped to avoid the mud.
But then I tripped and landed with a *thud!*
Oh no, I was stuck in a sticky, squelchy bog!

The man was coming fast, could he turn me into a frog?
I was doomed!
Then, the approaching man boomed,
"Wait, young sir, I have your shoe!
I didn't mean to scare you!
My cloak may look sinister, see,
But, in fact, it hides all we need for afternoon tea.
Now, let's get you out of this bog,
Hold onto this knobbly log."

With one yank of the wizard's hand,
I was back on dry land.
"Now, what was that bang?" I asked.
"It was a firework that made a blast."

"My animal friends must be scared.
I need to take them the tea I prepared.
You are invited to come along,
On the way, let's sing a song!"

Gosh! I thought happily, *my first impression was wrong.*
I ended up with a wonderful tea with the wizard's animal friends.
I'm so sad... this dream is coming to an end.

It's amazing to think that all is not always as it seems,
Once upon a dream!

Toby Webber (8)
Warminster Prep, Warminster

Witches Vs Fairies

I step into my bed, so springy, soft and deep,
I close my eyes and drift smoothly to sleep,
Suddenly, my room starts to fade,
Bright lights appear,
Then I hear,
Shouts, screams and cackles, filling my ear,
I realise when a ball whizzes by,
It's a netball match and fairies can fly,
It's fairies vs witches, and then I notice the fairies
are behind,
The witches are cheating with spells so unkind,
I see a flash of a wand,
And hear a big, crashing sound,
The crowd moans and groans,
But the coach calls my name,
I notice I am part of the team and we continue
the game,
I fly, catch and pass, now I'm part of the team,
The witches are frightened now,
We win and I'm living my dream,
I feel great and proud, but tired,
Then my wings start to fade,
My alarm starts to wail, beep and buzz,

So I open my eyes,
Back in bed, I am lying.

Isabella Thomas (8)
Warminster Prep, Warminster

Football Nightmare

I was at the field Camp Nou,
With my biggest idol, Neymar,
He stepped on me, and I felt blue,
Then I woke up and I was in a bar,
It was the Second World War,
And I was really scared and sore,
But I had a phone,
I called my friends at home,
They tried to find me,
But they didn't know where I was,
I thought I was stuck in there forever,
I heard a sound,
And it was a guard who wanted a catch,
But I woke up to my alarm and realised,
I was late for the Barcelona and Real Madrid match!

Albert Sjo (8)
Warminster Prep, Warminster

Minecraft

M any are the nights when I dream the same,

I love nothing more than this game.

N o one other than Ender Dragon is the boss,

E ndermen are tall, purple-eyed, and cross.

C reepers without arms explode at the sight of a cat,

R anger's neck extends, and his horns could wear a hat.

A xalotl change colour and live in a cave,

F ox is shy but, in a mob, is brave.

T onight, I expect I'll dream of Minecraft again.

Gray Williams (10)
Warminster Prep, Warminster

Scurry, Squeak

In the quiet with the soft light of the lamp
I lay and closed my eyes,
As the moon lights the skies.

A quiet, soft squeak I hear,
Rising from my sleep as the squeaking comes near.

A gentle waft of forest trees,
The feeling is rough on my knees.

I open my tired eyes and realise,
I am with the mice!

With my fur grey
I go off and play.

Scurry, squeak, scurry, squeak,
I hope this dream lasts all week...

Joshua Coll-Cats (8)
Warminster Prep, Warminster

The Magic Ponies

In the middle of the darkness,
There is a place of magic,
The only place where anything is possible,
And chestnut horses gallop,
Faster than the world can turn
And bluebells grow faster than any wind could fly,
This place is a dream,
No one has ever found this magical place,
Will someone find it one day?

Ariana Hare (8)
Warminster Prep, Warminster

Midnights

Darkness in my bedroom,
Oh how I wish I could escape the dark void.
Slowly I got out of bed,
As I felt a sharp pain in my head.
Crash! I fell to the ground,
As I heard a familiar sound.
As I opened my eyes I found,
A girl just like me, sobbing away.
I ask, "Why so down?"
She said, "I don't have any friends."
Silence in the room
I said, "Am I dreaming?"
She said, "Yes, but I don't want it to end."
I said, "What? Why? How come I'm here?"
She said, "You have been chosen."
The dream ended.
I woke up to my mum calling me for breakfast.
I said, "Five more minutes!"

Phoebe Handoll (8)
Welton Primary School, Midsomer Norton

Fairy Lands

F airy Land is the best place you can be,

A t Fairy Land, you are always filled with glee!

I like it because it's fun and you can run anywhere you like!

R ight when you step inside, you know you'll be there for a long time!

Y ou will think it's home even though it's your first time!

L ike always, they'll lock the gates at night so the nightmares don't get in.

A t night, you'll have the best dreams possible!

N o way you can leave this early!

D o stay, and maybe you'll just love it here.

S o if you are going, make sure to tell people to come here; we are very lonely!

Gabriella Monti (8)
Welton Primary School, Midsomer Norton

A Girl's Dream

A girl's dream was to be a teacher
And the students were little cheaters.
The teacher, as busy as bees,
The students surrounded her knees.

The teacher was teaching maths
Whilst a child was making crafts.
The teacher was teaching art,
But a student was bringing in darts.

The teacher said it was too sunny,
Whilst the children thought it was funny.
Finally, it was time for home.
But Evie thought she was alone.

The teacher finally got home
To see a garden gnome.
It's time for dinner,
Let's go and see your favourite singer.

Elsie Wood (9)
Welton Primary School, Midsomer Norton

Bugs Turn Big

My dog, Lucky, and I were walking along the dancing
grass,
The trees were moving and whispering as we walked
past.
In the forest, it was really hot,
I thought we were alone, but we were not.
We saw a pot that was very hot.
Next to the pot lay potions of all different colours.
We started putting potions into the dark mysterious
pot, which was so hot.
We started to mix the potions,
It started to giggle and wiggle,
A massive bug jumped out,
He looked friendly,
So I started to stroke him.
He followed us,
I said that maybe he could live with us.

William Hall (8)
Welton Primary School, Midsomer Norton

Battlefields

I'm running through a battlefield,
Lots of these fields are filled with reels.

The splattering rain is hitting my legs,
Like they're getting poured with kegs.

Mud sticking on my knees,
Nearby lightning striking thee.

Down comes a crow,
Now I wonder where I am, of course, I don't know!

Right now, it's a terrible storm,
I hope it comes after dawn!

Thunder and lightning are in the air,
It's even worse because I'm in the middle of nowhere.

Jake Carroll (9)
Welton Primary School, Midsomer Norton

Magic Monsters

I sneak away from home,
Not knowing where to go,
I hear a funny noise,
And I feel myself poise,
In order to prepare,
For whatever is there.

I see some food,
And I'm in the mood,
I try to take it,
But there is something big.

A dragon awakens,
I am mistaken,
I wish I stayed at home,
Instead of being alone.

The monsters come out to play,
I wish there was another way,
The monsters are nice,
And they don't want to fight.

Amber Dires (9)
Welton Primary School, Midsomer Norton

Going To Wizard School

While on the train, I'm very excited,
Eating the food, I'm very delighted,
Trying new clothes, potions and spells,
Seeing outside and very deep wells,
In the halls, I'm going to class,
Inside the class, there is very green grass,
In the sky, I can see a unicorn,
With a very sharp horn,
Wizard School is the best place you can be,
And it fills you up with glee,
The first day of Wizard School was fun,
Nobody should ever be glum.

India Makombe (9)
Welton Primary School, Midsomer Norton

Deadly Dragons

In a forest far away,
It was a very cold day,
The dragon had very hot breath,
And had eaten a very good chef.

When he met a monster chilling in the water,
And he also ate a quarter,
So he made a big laughter,
And suddenly flew straight after.

When my brother came with an axe,
I spotted something shiny on the axe, it was wax,
We came up with a scheme to defeat the dragon,
And he said to himself, "I made a wagon."

Max Risdale (8)
Welton Primary School, Midsomer Norton

The Monster

At midnight, in the city,
On the road, I saw a kitty.
Suddenly, something yanked the kitty.
I saw a monster, it was very creepy

The monster was hairy,
His name was Mary.
It was old and blood red.
Its teeth were like knives.

Suddenly, it tried to grab me!
But, it failed.
Then it started to hit me,
Then it disappeared somewhere.
I still have not seen it!

Isaac Dular (8)
Welton Primary School, Midsomer Norton

Swimming

Big and deep,
And light blue,
Into the shining pool
I flew.

Under the water,
I begin to glide,
Whilst my big sister
Goes down the slide.

I swim around
Blowing out as I go,
Now it's time to get out,
I'm Mr Grouch.

After we go to the park,
I play around,
Until I see a lark,
Now I'm warm.

Rory Cottle (9)
Welton Primary School, Midsomer Norton

Space

It was a normal day in space,
I had a happy face,
There were hoover-like black holes.

I was weightless,
And I felt fateless,
As I floated through the air.

I waved at the black,
But no one waved back,
And the loneliness made me feel sad.

I saw rocks,
That seem to knock,
Into each other,
At lightning bolt speed.

Max Button (8)
Welton Primary School, Midsomer Norton

The Universe

You can see it flickering like fire,
How it moves at 1000km per hour,
Can you see how it moves?

The black hole, can you hear it?
The millions of galaxies can you see them?
All the googolplexians of atoms.

All the heat from stars like boiling water,
But hotter,
What else is there to do?
Except see this through.

Marley Bugler (9)
Welton Primary School, Midsomer Norton

My Cat And I

My cat and I were in my house,
We were very still, as silent as a mouse.
Very quiet, we crept
And silently, we wept.

In a room with my cat,
I saw something, it was a bat.
Suddenly I felt full of might,
And then I struck a light.

Now my cat and I set a scheme,
We both woke up; it was all a dream.

Lilah Toogood (9)
Welton Primary School, Midsomer Norton

Colours And Planets

Colours and planets all around space,
I am floating all around the place,
My friends float around me,
It's the only happiness I see,
Looking at all of the colours,
I see lots of lovers.

Look at all of the planets gleaming,
Look around, the sun is beaming.

Gesa Surocaj (8)
Welton Primary School, Midsomer Norton

Bath Rugby

R ugby balls kicked up high,
U nder a cloudy blue sky.
G asping fans, with a try.
B ath Rugby is the best!
Y ellow and red, worn on their chest. Go, Bath, go!

Bradley Adams (8)
Welton Primary School, Midsomer Norton

Pirate Sloths

I'm dreaming of the pirate sloths that roam the
Atlantic Sea,
One stormy night they captured me, and the other
three.
They wore pirate hats and long black cloaks,
They really did look scary until they finally spoke.

They said, "Please don't worry, we are not bad,
We need help from you, Leo, and your mum and dad.
We only have this broken map to locate the treasure."
I reply, "Yes, we'll help. It'll be our pleasure."

We travelled for miles across stormy seas,
All night and all day on the ocean breeze.
We find the treasure on a desert island,
Rubies, pearls, silver and a huge diamond.

Then, with a jump, I woke up in my bed,
It was just a dream, it was all in my head.

Logan Nelder (10)
William De Yaxley CE Academy, Yaxley

New York!

I like to eat pie
Banana pie

With sprinkles and whipped cream
This girl had a dream

She awoke with a scream
Her suitcase was nowhere to be seen

I found a magic potion
It looked like lotion

I took a big drink
Then suddenly I shrink

I climbed in the case
And made base

The suitcase took off
It went to New York

Oops, wrong flight!
The passengers above me are having a fight

I blocked out the noise
And played with some toys

I found out the suitcase was magic
That was tragic

I went to New York
And ate some pork

I was playing around
But suddenly a frown

Where's my pie?
Someone lied

And said they hadn't seen my pie
But I was fine
I still had a life.

Peggy Minns (10)
William De Yaxley CE Academy, Yaxley

Ben The Great And Friends

B efore the big bang
E nchanted lands built by Ben and friends
N othing new or old, only half.

T imes were fun,
H aving a great time,
E njoying the moment, but,

G reat monsters ruled the land and killed people,
R uled the land like monsters.
E than fought the beast but sadly passed,
A nd the crowd was upset but two exited the crowd
and said they would fight,
T hey are called Ben and Emily.

F amous in the world,
R eign country with no fear,
I am powerful, they are powerful,
E nd the monster, dead, killed, gone.
N othing but fun left,
D one, no one left but me and her.

Ben Woods (10)
William De Yaxley CE Academy, Yaxley

Untitled

One silent night
I was in Ukraine and we were like
No, no, the fight will not start
And I wake up and I hear
Umm, umm,
That is the sound
For when we have to go to a safe place,
That means the war has started.
I was crying,
My hands were shaking,
And we went to my grandma and grandad
Because they had a secret safe place.
Then we were there two months
And going to the Polshia,
There were my cousins and my other grandma.
We were there three months
And have gone to England, my mum said
Just for three weeks,
We went there because there
Was my dad's sister
And now we are here
For one year,
I'm really sad.

Marta Bilous (10)
William De Yaxley CE Academy, Yaxley

Where I Belong...

Far far away, on a beach, where the sea was as clear as glass.

The sun shone and the waves were crashing on the soft sand.

While people jumped into the sea, boats passed the swimmers and lifeguards sat high, waiting to help.

A cat passed me as I sat on a towel under a bright-coloured umbrella.

The cat kept coming back, so it could tell me something.

I followed the cat, curiously. The cat had a white fur coat.

Looking up at something I hadn't seen since I was seven, was a house I had pictured before.

I walked in, seeing a line of cats making a pathway I could cross.

I walked into a portal, it closed behind me.

I realised I was in the place I belonged, a paradise, more than a dream.

Yazmyn Bruce (11)
William De Yaxley CE Academy, Yaxley

Red Dress

The dream I had last night,
Something didn't feel quite right.
It felt like my feet were glued to this very strange house,
There was no sound, it was as quiet as a mouse.

Just as I froze,
The tension rose.
I felt a doze but could not go to sleep,
It was my wildest dream.

My heart was racing
As I ran up the stairs,
Into the murky air.
Where am I, just where?

The water rising, my suspicion multiplying
A lady stood there in a red dress.
Red like blood.
And *thud!*

That was my head as I woke up in bed,
It was the middle of the night,
I picked up my teddy and
Snuggled up tight.

Mary-Jayne Mortlock (10)
William De Yaxley CE Academy, Yaxley

All Alone

I'm in my house all alone
I set up blankets and pillows for a throne.
With my television, and teddies by my side
I feel excitement, I cannot hide.

I watch a movie, snuggly and cosy
Building my den is really rosy.
But all of a sudden a gust of wind
My den gets blown, it has been binned.

I start again with determination
Embracing the unexpected situation.
In the end my den stands proud
A cosy haven away from the crowd.

But in the shadows, something caught my eye
A mysterious figure looming made me sigh.
But as it came closer, I really could see
That it was my loyal dog Max bringing me a cup of tea!

Daisy Meighan (10)
William De Yaxley CE Academy, Yaxley

The Forest Full Of Guinea Pigs

I woke up in a forest,
I looked up and all I could see were green leaves,
Dangling off beautiful trees,
I stood surrounded by wood,
I thought I was alone,
Everywhere was overgrown,
Then squeaking and purring caught my attention,
I followed the noises and saw peeking noses,
Lots of guinea pigs scuttling about,
Two seemed to stand out,
I picked them up and put them in my pocket,
I foraged for food, finding them fruit and berries,
We cuddled together for what felt like forever,
I named them Isadora and Gizmo,
Then I woke to realise this was all a dream,
I really felt upset and I wanted to scream.

Jessica Bailey (10)
William De Yaxley CE Academy, Yaxley

In My Mythical Mind Dreams

With my flying horse
I can see the whole mythical world
Flapping its wings up near the clouds that swirl.

Monsters in the alleyway
Shouting and screaming all day
With the big sharp claws
It's hard to open doors
They always have quite big claws

Scary wizards in their cloaks
All the potions make them soaked
Surrounded by frogs that croak
They always have a little joke

Dragons with their fiery breath
They sometimes have a tragic death
With their siblings they always fight
It sometimes ends with a bite
I was cautious looking down
Taking photos all around.

Sophie Balaam (8)
William De Yaxley CE Academy, Yaxley

Spider And Monster, Dragons And Pirates And Fairies

Spiders are big and they live in webs.
Monsters are under beds,
They are wild.
Football is fun.
Pirates are rich, all of them are rich.
Dragons breathe fire,
They breathe and destroy homes with fire.
If you look closely fairies hide until you're not watching
Or it's too dark to use their superpowers
To take your teeth from your pillows or hide your keys or toys.
What's more scary, spiders and monsters, dragons and pirates, or fairies?
For me, it's fairies with superpowers
As they are small little things
And sometimes can be scary.
Avoid superpowered fairies at all costs!

Harper Devon (7)
William De Yaxley CE Academy, Yaxley

Local Heroes

N ewcastle United feels like home to me,
E veryone loves the Toon,
W ith excitement and joy the crowd roars,
C allum Wilson scores the final goal before half-time,
A penalty is given,
S cores!
T he crowd goes wild when Trippier scores,
L ast two minutes before the final whistle blows,
E veryone is silent,

U nited we stand,
N othing left to do, Newcastle wins!
I t's a dream come true,
T he trophy gets held by the team,
E xcitement on the player's faces,
D reams do come true.

Violet Hunter (9)
William De Yaxley CE Academy, Yaxley

The FA Cup

The cool, crisp air,
Fans cheering everywhere,
Red and white all ready to fight,
My boots are green and black,
Running fast from the back,
Jumped up high almost touching the sky,
For a split second, I thought I could fly,
Wind in my face, what a pace,
A rainbow flick and a flip-flap trick,
Dodging defenders so nervous,
My heat popped out of my soul,
With the end in sight, the goalkeeper put up a fight,
With a nutmeg, I scored the winning goal,
I hold up the FA Cup,
My chest is thumping with pride,
What a ride!
Oh, how I wish I was a football player.

Connor Dickson (9)
William De Yaxley CE Academy, Yaxley

Great Grandad

G reat Grandad is someone who we love.
R ecently he has been watching us from above.
E veryone misses him.
A lso, he was a great man.
T aking care of everyone is what he wants us to do.

G rateful to have all of the memories.
R emember him forever and ever.
A lways, any time I feel sad, he will comfort me.
N ow I'll think of him every day.
D on't ever want this moment to go away.
A bsolute legend is what you are.
D on't ever leave me. I think of you every time I see a star.

Sonny Rooney (10)
William De Yaxley CE Academy, Yaxley

Dream In Spring

I sat on my balcony alone,
Watching the magical trees below,
I wondered when the flowers will grow,
But hey, I guess we'll never know,
One by one, the birds fly by,
Where I'm watching with an eye.
Now I'm wondering, *is this a dream?*
The trees are like diamonds, and the stars look like treats.
I see a mysterious animal that glistens in the nebula sky,
I went downstairs to go see it,
But sadly it went.
Maybe next time I can sneak up on it,
Like a spy.
Suddenly, I woke up in my bed.
My mum telling me to get ready for school.

Thaian Hoang (11)
William De Yaxley CE Academy, Yaxley

Taking Flight

I'm weightless, I'm free,
I'm higher than the trees,
I'm soaring, it's Disney,
Right in front of me,
I see Donald, I see Goofy,
I see Mickey, I see Minnie,
I look down, they look up,
They smile and wave at me.

The rides and the food stands all look like fun,
Even when the day is done,
As I fly up in the sky,
Me and Peter meet eye-to-eye,
He smiles and takes my hand,
And tells me, "We're going to Neverland."

The stars and moon shine so bright,
On the night, we were taking flight.

Skylar Paterson (9)
William De Yaxley CE Academy, Yaxley

A World Of Light

Once, in my dream, I saw a world of light,
The sun shone bright, and the moon lit up the night,
The stars twinkled, and the sky was clear,
The wind whispered secrets, and I could hear.

The trees danced like they were turned,
Their leaves rustled, and their branches crooned,
The world was alive, and I was free,
To explore and discover, what I could see.

So beautiful, though just a dream,
Seemed so real, but then it was unseen,
But, in my heart, I know it's true,
Although I can't go back,
At least I won't be blue.

Alicja Skowronska (11)
William De Yaxley CE Academy, Yaxley

Terrors

She kissed me to sleep,
Before I knew what would reap,
It was cold and filled with mould,
When the Grim Reaper said,
"Welcome to your terror,"
He had his sharpened scythe,
And was ready to take me to Hell.

The fire burned my skin,
And I was calling for help,
But then,
Standing at the top, breathing heavily,
Skyscrapers touch the clouds,
Feeling my face, an empty space,
No teeth chatter or chew,
Creeping in the dark, feeling their way,
A venomous bite,
Heartbeat racing,
Dreams that awaken me.

Jack Wright (11)
William De Yaxley CE Academy, Yaxley

Noises

Every noise inside my head
Keeps me on the surface ahead,
I like the world full of steam,
It keeps me flowing on the stream.

I love a quiet place,
It makes me calm and straight.
As the wind flies by,
The sky sings a lullaby.

To the sly lives that live in the nights,
An act of kindness could bring light,
And an act of sorrow could shine bright.

The noise that rings between your ears,
Could get rid of your fears,
So make sure it's right,
To be the famous light
That sees what you could be.

Beau Mills (9)
William De Yaxley CE Academy, Yaxley

A Brother

A dream I've had for a very long time is for Mum to have another baby,

B aby? She says no, not yet, maybe get another pet,
R unning with my sisters is lots of fun, wish I had another one,
O ver and over, I begged again, but the answer was the same,
T hen on Christmas night, Mum told me my dream would be a reality,
H ow happy it made me that Mum was having another baby,
E xcited one dream came true, I asked for another,
R unning to Mum I asked, "Please can it be a little brother?"

Bradley Holland (10)
William De Yaxley CE Academy, Yaxley

Nature Is All Around Us

The sun rose
The water flows
Birds were singing in the meadows
Birds in the sky flying so high
Stars like crystals in the sky
So beautiful I might cry
Flowers by day, stars by night
Why can't they just reunite?
Spring came along, but not for long
The blossom on the trees grew back so fast
Summer came so strong
The flowers grew too long
Autumn came along
By then all flowers were gone
Snow is falling, snowmen and snowballs all around
Money is dropping
Because it is time to celebrate all around.

Isla Barber (9)
William De Yaxley CE Academy, Yaxley

A World Of Chocolate

Once upon a dream,
A boy made a teleporting machine,
It took him to a world which was magical, it
would seem,
Full of candy, sweets, chocolate and cream,
He found a chocolate fountain where he then sat,
Fully ready to scoff until he got fat,
Bunnies were hopping with chocolate for ears,
This was a great dream with no fears,
Is that a gumdrop button in place of the sun?
Is it the moon or a chocolate bun?
The little boy was actually just me,
I don't want to wake up yet,
There is so much more to eat and see.

Isaac Coker (10)
William De Yaxley CE Academy, Yaxley

What Should I Do?

What should I do, oh, what should I do?
Athletics is my life, but football is just the same.
Elizabeth is saying "Choose Athletics."
But Daisy is saying "Choose football."
I need to make my decision
Because time is running out,
I can't escape this despicable nightmare,
Nothing has prepared me for this stressful decision.
I look left and right but all I see is athletics and
football.
When suddenly, there is a crash!
I'm back in my bed, lying awake.
I never want to have a bad dream again.

Lily Legg (10)
William De Yaxley CE Academy, Yaxley

Revival Of British Railways

B eneath the stars, a night so bright,

R iding rails is pure delight.

I n a world where everything is alive,

T hrough valleys and hills where nature thrives.

I hear trains that hum a rhythmic theme.

S urely this can't be a dream.

H uge, grand stations, sometimes hiding,

R ails running into sidings.

A Pullman carriage and a flatbed truck,

I 'm lying comfortably, reading my book.

L ocomotives have no rival, surely I can start the revival.

Jenson Vellam (11)
William De Yaxley CE Academy, Yaxley

The Real Me

In a magical world in the mountains, high above the clouds...
Lived a happy young girl called Eva, who had a secret she was dying to tell...
"I am a dragon!" she shouted at the top of her voice...
A flying, soaring dragon, a lightning dragon, a black, gold, and flashing dragon...
A lightning-breath dragon, a cool dragon, a fun dragon...
I-wish-I-had-some-friends dragon!
It's lonely being a dragon, I wish I could just tell someone,
But would they be afraid of me, the real me,
The dragon me and not just little Eva?

Emmie Guy (11)
William De Yaxley CE Academy, Yaxley

Shadow Show At Night

When birds are snuggled into trees,
When night begins to fall,
My hand makes shadows,
In the spaces on my wall.

The moon flutters in my window,
Like a glowing eye,
To help my hands turn into birds and bugs,
And flapping fingers fly.

My hands are dogs and dragons,
I learn new shapes each night,
Shadow-shapes of cats and dogs,
Dance through the silky sky.

My hands feel calm and steady,
When making forests and sky,
Birds flutter through my window,
In the shiny summer sky.

Ruby Eaton (11)
William De Yaxley CE Academy, Yaxley

Dancing Free

D reams of dancing fill my head,

A round my family and all my friends.

N ervous if I fall or if it ends.

C hecking left and right, ready to take flight.

I lluminating stage lights get more bright,

N avigating around the stage.

G uaranteed a big parade.

F or this is what my dream would be,

R avishing dresses, shine in glee.

E mbelished in the finest jewellery.

E nding the dream, I am so depressed, awakening from rest.

Madison-Rae Scott (11)

William De Yaxley CE Academy, Yaxley

The Enchanted Forest

Fairies flying all around us,
talking and singing joyfully.
In the moonlight of the forest,
we are all looking for the fairy king.

Me, MJ, and Florence mesmerised by the enchanted
forest,
with its glistening trees and sparkling streams.
With its colourful birds flying above,
singing its beautiful songs.

And all the animals dancing
in the enchanted forest,
we all look high and low for the fairy king.

But sadly, he was nowhere to be seen,
maybe next time.

Amelia Ayres (11)
William De Yaxley CE Academy, Yaxley

Street Dance

S trutting my stuff on stage
T oo many people whizzing about
R epetitive rhythms floating in my mind
E veryone rushing to get ready to perform
E yes all on us from the crowd
T rying my best to remember the routine

D are I dance in front of everyone?
A lways trying my best to show off my moves
N othing has prepared me for this moment
C an feel butterflies in my tummy
E veryone is cheering as I do my final pose.

Summer Ivens (8)
William De Yaxley CE Academy, Yaxley

Everybody's Different

You don't need to be perfect,
You just need to try.
So wash away those grumpy days,
And end up on a high.

You don't need to smile,
To show that you're okay.
But as long as you're happy,
It won't be a rainy day.

Everyone is different,
In their own way.
So just be yourself,
And have a good day.

Cool as a cucumber,
No worries on your mind.
But as long as you're adventurous,
There are things that you can find.

Poppy Maxwell (10)
William De Yaxley CE Academy, Yaxley

A World Of Wizards

When I go to sleep
My eyes begin to close
My brain starts to dream
About something nobody else knows
I'm in a dream world full of magical wizards
The weather is very very cold
So they rush me inside
Away from the blizzards
I'm now in a castle all cosy and warm
As I drink my hot cocoa
I get to see all the magic
The wizards perform
I'm so excited to see all of the magic
And I ask to partake
But as soon as I get up and join
I suddenly awake!

Harvey Searle (9)
William De Yaxley CE Academy, Yaxley

Space Cows

In my dreams every night,
Space cows float with colour galore,
Neon tails and vivid blue ears,
Floating and spinning all around space.
One by one, they pass me by,
In the midnight starry sky.
The lead cows fly high in the air,
Scattering shooting stars from their feet,
From a big way away from Earth,
They've come to space to make a bond.
Every night I leave out hay,
Hoping that they would stay,
But sadly, they disappear,
For now until next year.

Gabia Datas (9)
William De Yaxley CE Academy, Yaxley

A Nice Summer Day On The Beach

The little waves of the water,
Ripple over the thirsty sand.
The little shaft of sunlight,
Sail off to distant lands.
Like the clouds wandering in the ocean-blue sky,
I take a stroll on the sandy beach.
When I hear the sea roaring wildly,
I stop and look at the sea,
Gentle swaying to the ocean breeze.
I wish summer would never end,
But to school, I must attend.
I miss you, summer,
But I won't fuss,
I'll see you soon, in ten months plus.

Teshia Christopher (11)
William De Yaxley CE Academy, Yaxley

Once Upon A Dream

As the trees swayed in the breeze,
The horses galloped.
While the horses galloped,
In the soil was a worm with no eyes which was very adventurous.
While it wriggled through the soil it started to rain,
And the birds came.
The birds can fly all around,
To eat the worms right off the ground.
The worm swam throughout the lake,
Jumping around on buckets and leaves.
Then all at once the rain stopped,
And the birds flew back into the branches of the trees.

Tyler Johnson (11)
William De Yaxley CE Academy, Yaxley

Bertie And The Stars

I lay sleeping soundly in bed,
Drifting away with a mask on my head.
In my dream, I was far, far away.
Somewhere very dark,
It could be any other day.

In my dream, I'm sitting with stars.
Looking down on the Earth and across at Mars.
I think I'm alone and start to feel scared.

Then my dog, Bertie, appears, and I have no fears.
As he leaps with glee, too happy to see me.
I woke up in bed with him sitting on my head.

Florence Connolly (10)
William De Yaxley CE Academy, Yaxley

Sheep Dreams

When I close my eyes and drift away,
I find myself standing in the hay.
I try to tell myself to walk,
But realise that I can't talk.

When I opened my mouth to scream,
I knew that I was in a dream.
This happens every time I sleep,
And after a while, I see some sheep.

I see the sheep come up to me,
They make me want to sing in glee.
Suddenly, my clock goes beep!
Next time I sleep, I'll see the sheep.

Ellie-Rose Taylor (11)
William De Yaxley CE Academy, Yaxley

Doug The Slug

I had a dream that I bought a slug,
When I got home, I named him Doug.
I found out he could talk, which gave me quite a shock,
I gave him a bed, which was made out of a sock.
He told me carrots were his favourite food, so I got some from the shop,
But he could not eat a whole bunch. I told him he had to stop!
Doug was a friendly, brown, slimy slug,
Although he was not the best at giving a hug.
One day, he fell into a pot of cream,
Then I woke up, and it was all a dream.

Joshua Pleasance (10)
William De Yaxley CE Academy, Yaxley

All Comes Down To This...

Football I love
You can't beat it bruv.
The feeling I get,
When the ball hits the net.
Like I'm flying high,
Right up in the sky.
My head's in the game,
My teammate's the same.
The whistle blows,
Two minutes to go.
One more goal we need,
To finally succeed.
I get the ball,
The defender falls.
The front of the net,
This goal we must get.
The ball goes in,
Yes! We win!

Noah Giles (10)
William De Yaxley CE Academy, Yaxley

Marvellous Dreams!

Lying in my bed one night,
Mysterious sounds enter my mind.
Into Dreamland, here I come,
What else to see but a sugar plum?
Lots of mushroom houses,
Stories and poems everywhere.
Crystal caves,
A fellow sugar plum comes up to me
And tells me face-to-face
We need to find the Necklace of Epiphany.
Through the Hazelnut Forest,
I see a crystal cave.
We go inside to see
The Necklace of Epiphany.

Robin Buckingham (8)
William De Yaxley CE Academy, Yaxley

Out In The Garden

One day in the glossy, bright moon
I saw a floating balloon.
To my surprise, I saw my friend, Maylee,
Floating by.

She joined me in the shiny, bright stars.

We had the best time ever,
But I heard a boom,
And it was coming from my room.

We went to my room,
And the boom was loud,
And it got louder and louder.

And it was...
My new toy!

The end of my dream.

Autumn Donachie (8)
William De Yaxley CE Academy, Yaxley

The Feather

F inding myself in dreamland when I fall asleep,
E verywhere I go, I see feathers floating in the air,
A s I look around, all I can see is feathers,
T he feathers make me feel magical when I see them,
H oping the feathers won't blow away,
E very feather, as light as can be,
R unning through the feathers, trying to catch them,
S eems like the dream is endless.

Elsie Everett (9)
William De Yaxley CE Academy, Yaxley

Athlete Superpower

A ctive
T rack sports
H ealthy
L ong-distance running
E nergetic
T eamwork
E xciting

S uper, amazing
U p in the air
P owers are shocking
E xciting
R eally fun
P owers are amazing
O vercoming fears
W ith a team
E scape
R adioactive
S hocking.

Katie Clarke (8)
William De Yaxley CE Academy, Yaxley

Creepy Circus In The Night

In the night, every night,
I see monsters all through the night,
Swishing, twirling everywhere,
They come to give you a scare.
Be ready,
Oh! It's my teddy bear on the chair.
I didn't know I was scared of my teddy bear!
Wait, wait, what's that I hear?
It's the growl of the monster that's under my bed,
Mummy, Mummy, I'm scared of the monster that's under my bed.

Henry Smith (7)
William De Yaxley CE Academy, Yaxley

A Cat In My Bed

My neighbour's cat is called Jumpy.
He's always friendly, not grumpy.
At night he flies through my door.
Landing with a thump on the floor.
With a loud meow and a big purr.
He jumps on my bed, moulting fur.
My brother, Logan and I are very pleased.
We stroke Jumpy and give him a squeeze.
He sleeps in my bed for a couple of hours
And then flies back out using his superpowers.

Jack Nelder (8)
William De Yaxley CE Academy, Yaxley

My Dog, Bella

B ella the dog is so very cute,
E ven when she's guarding her precious loot,
L ittle Bella likes all her toys,
L ittle Bella barks to make some noise,
A nd Bella is the cutest one,

Even when she's barking on,
But then I woke up just to see,
In front of me, there was no cute puppy,
And it makes me sad that I...
I just really want to cry.

Harvey Renno (10)
William De Yaxley CE Academy, Yaxley

Royalty

In a kingdom where the crown gleams,
A ruler reigns, majestic in every way.
With grace and poise, they guide the way,
Guiding their people through the day.

Their kingdom flourishes under their rule,
Their wisdom and kindness, a precious jewel.
Radiating warmth, like a fire that's fuelled.
In their presence, hearts are high,
Their guidance and love, never saying goodbye.

Lexi Earl (11)
William De Yaxley CE Academy, Yaxley

An Artist's Dream

Sitting at the table with my paintbrush in my hand,
I paint pictures of polar bears in an icy land,
Sitting at the table with my felt tips in my hand,
Colouring pictures of pyramids in the sand,
Sitting at the table, with my pencils in my hand,
Drawing monsters and animals from a faraway land,
My paper is full of many colours and designs,
Lots of shapes, patterns and squiggly lines.

Ryan Wright (7)
William De Yaxley CE Academy, Yaxley

Spiders

"S it," said a voice I had never heard
 P atting me on the head like the wings of a bird
  I looked around to find the noise, but nothing could be seen
 D eep inside the darkness, I heard a terrifying scream
 E choing around the room was an eerie crawling sound
 R eaching for the light, I was unprepared for what I found
 S *piders!*

Carter Williams (10)
William De Yaxley CE Academy, Yaxley

Hack In The Clouds

I drift to sleep
And all I hear
Is the sound of your gallop
As you race and rear.

The wind through your mane
And the swoosh in your tail
As I mount on board
I know we can't fail.

We canter away a summer set
I take a deep breath and there's nothing too great
Your hooves that dance on the clouds above
A dream of freedom and endless love.

Lily Forsythe (10)
William De Yaxley CE Academy, Yaxley

The Lost Soul

I met a monster on a cliff,
While I was reading a hieroglyph.
The monster was big and tall,
Standing on a massive wall.

With its strongest blow,
It would send me six feet below.
Then at once, a city appeared,
Shrouded in smoke, the monster fled as the
castle neared.

I was a little scared; I started to scream,
Then I awoke; it was a dream.

Aidan Vellam (11)
William De Yaxley CE Academy, Yaxley

Monsters

M y car suddenly ran out of fuel and stopped,

O n this dark night at midnight,

N ever before had I felt more afraid,

S uddenly, in the distance, shapes were moving in the shadows,

T rees were waving their sharp branches,

E ventually, I see brightness in the distance,

R escuers arrive with their flashing lights,

S aved!

Dylan Tyler (10)
William De Yaxley CE Academy, Yaxley

I Got Lost

I 'm starting to get nervous.

G oing places I don't know.
O ut of my comfort zone.
T he more I walk, the further I get from home.

L ots and lots of nerves are on end.
O ver the moon and under the stars, I shall go.
S earching for home but avoiding danger.
T ight in my chest and deep in my dream.

Mair Powell (9)
William De Yaxley CE Academy, Yaxley

The Dragon

Once upon a time, there lived a builder
And he was cursed in the worst way
If he doesn't get saved from the dancer
He will become an evil dragon
And you will never see him again
And the dancer lived in the Netherlands
And she got a text message from the builder
So she was on her way, but she was too late.
They married
And lived happily ever after.

Elsie Woods (8)
William De Yaxley CE Academy, Yaxley

No Escape

N ight falls when all is silent.
O nly a girl and a boy aren't going to be violent.

E ntering the woods,
S tood them in their hoods.
C alling for animals
A nd suddenly, they heard vandals.
P eeling was heard, then drops of liquid and running.
E nding the story, it's gory with gunning.

Henry Ford (10)
William De Yaxley CE Academy, Yaxley

Locked In

Locked inside and out,
I am tempted to shout.
But it would be no use
Because breath I will lose.
No windows, just a door,
No one to save me anymore.

It is like someone is blocking the door,
Making sure I cannot escape.
"Someone save me, for God's sake!"
As my oxygen depletes.
My time of living will be ceased.

Harvey Thain (11)
William De Yaxley CE Academy, Yaxley

My Dream

F rom the start, I knew what I wanted
O n the field, I practised and approached
O ne day my dream will come true
T hey all come to watch me
B right lights shining
A ll I need is to do my best
L ife will be good
L ife will be grand
E njoy this day
R emember this forever.

Jacob Leger (9)
William De Yaxley CE Academy, Yaxley

Best Friend

Lily is my best friend each year,
She helps me,
She helps me through each year,
Many, many times,
She makes sure I never get hurt,
Each time she brings me happiness,
When I am sad she always comforts me,
Each year she will always help me through,
She sometimes can be a really funny person,
But she is a really nice person to me.

Elizabeth Mallory (10)
William De Yaxley CE Academy, Yaxley

Cornwall: The Place I Dream Of

Cornwall in my dreams every night,
White tips and seagulls I see,
The waves crashing in the distance,
Each grain of sand between my toes,
Dogs chasing balls against the damp sand,
The scent of fish and chips is sensational
But pasties are the best delicacy,
Ocean waves running along our feet,
Surfers crumbling into the waves.

Emily Gingell (10)
William De Yaxley CE Academy, Yaxley

Take A Ride

I'm a little fairy, I like flying everywhere
I love going into the forest because my friends
are there.
Up in the treetops, down in the glen
Everyone loves being there.
Because we are all friends.
Hop onto a dragonfly and take a ride.
You won't know where you're going
Until the dragonfly decides.

Lacey Wheeler (11)
William De Yaxley CE Academy, Yaxley

On The Beach

Sand is on the land,
Shells and stones in my hand.
Crabs are mad, pinching stones,
Throwing them into the ocean.

The waves are swaying,
Speckled pebbles around,
While fish and turtles can be found.

Buckets and spades in the shade,
Waiting for me to come and play,
Before the sun goes down.

Tyler Darby (7)
William De Yaxley CE Academy, Yaxley

Minecraft

M inecraft is my favourite game,
I see villagers and go home,
N etherite cannot be tamed,
E ndermen are made,
C acti are wild,
R avagers are insane,
A nimals are to blame,
F iring arrows are the same,
T urtles are always getting named.

Jacob Christopher Turnell (10)
William De Yaxley CE Academy, Yaxley

Dreaming

D eep in my head, while I'm sleeping in bed
R emembering memories of my life
E specially my family and friends
A dventures and fun times we have
M y life whizzes by
I start to wake up
N ever wanting my dreams to end
G reat times fill my head.

Gracie Walton (11)
William De Yaxley CE Academy, Yaxley

The Scariest Dream

The scariest dream of my life
Came to me in just one night.
The monsters of doom
Made me gloom.
While the trees nuzzled
And the leaves rustled.
The roars of their threat made me sweat
And their eyes turned red after we met.
They had sharp claws on their paws
But they had no jaws.

Poppy Lenton (9)
William De Yaxley CE Academy, Yaxley

Trucking Down The Road

T aking my truck
R eady for spraying
U nder bridges, ready to duck
C hecking the load, no delaying
K eep on going. Exhaust is smoking
I 'm heading down the road
N early there, no time for joking
G et off that heavy load.

Oliver Dayman (11)
William De Yaxley CE Academy, Yaxley

The Crash

C limbed in my dad's van with my brother
R oads winding and weaving in the countryside
A argh! We are about to crash, stop!
S *mash! Bang!* My ears were ringing, then all of a
  sudden, it stopped
H urt and upset, we were lying amongst the rubble.

Freddie Lock (10)
William De Yaxley CE Academy, Yaxley

The Greatest Dancers

Every night as I lie in bed,
The greatest dancers fill my head.
They're dancing with pride as the crowd cheers.
The crowds are wowed, the lights are bright
As the dancers dance into the night.
Suddenly, I realise it is me!
Alongside the other dancers, happy as can be.

Sophie Toomey (9)
William De Yaxley CE Academy, Yaxley

The Darkness

Dreaming of lying in a dark, mysterious pit

As I wander around I just feel like it goes on and on
Running and running I start to realise
It's not a pit it's an endless loop of nothing
Kicking around the dust
Finding my way through this endless loop.

Ethan Everett (11)
William De Yaxley CE Academy, Yaxley

Flying

F un expiring, flying around the world.
L earning to fly, is an amazing dream.
Y et another dream to come.
I t feels silly, but it's not really.
N ight-time is the best time to dream.
G oing to fly is the best experience.

Harley Littlechild (10)
William De Yaxley CE Academy, Yaxley

Once They All Believed In Dragons

Once, they all believed in dragons.
When the world was young.
Tales were sung.
We were woven into Legend's Path.
We were treated with obedience.
We were honoured, we were feared.
But once they realised we were dragons
We were real!

Arijus Gintauskas (10)
William De Yaxley CE Academy, Yaxley

Wandered In Dream

As I wander lonely in a dream
Never to be seen
I'm tired of the full-beam sun
If I say one word, I'm gone

As I wander lonely in a dream
As I cannot be seen
By 7am I wake up and see I'm safe and seen
Always to be me.

Victoria Shinyanbola (11)
William De Yaxley CE Academy, Yaxley

178

Make-Up Artist, Make-Up Artist, Make my Dream Come True

Make-up artist, make-up artist
Make my dreams come true
With your big beautiful blue eyes
And your pink blushing cheeks
Red lips to die for
And your forehead clear as a trophy
And hair so blonde, so good
Please make my dreams come true
Like a little fairy.

Emily-Rose Nightingale (7)
William De Yaxley CE Academy, Yaxley

Basketball Dream

Myself, Leo D and Leo C meet LeBron James.
We walk to a basketball court.
It's the Staples Centre sports arena!
It's where the Los Angeles Lakers play.
We have a game.
I fly over the top of LeBron.
I shoot and score!

Zack Barton (10)
William De Yaxley CE Academy, Yaxley

Flowers Are All Different

Roses are red
Violets are blue
All flowers are different
Like you
Flowers blossom and bloom
In the middle of spring
Daisies are bright
Like humour
And sunflowers are fun to watch
Grow and blossom in the sun.

Sienna Devon (10)
William De Yaxley CE Academy, Yaxley

Never-Ending

In my dreams every night, I end up on a bridge,
Someone pushed me off, I didn't know them.
I fell and fell - it never ended,
It would always be falling and falling
And that's how it goes, it's just never-ending.

Leo Davidson (10)
William De Yaxley CE Academy, Yaxley

My Fruity Story

There was a yellow fellow
A banana went far in a car
I blinked in my eyes
And I saw banana pies
An orange, an orange scooter
A kiwi with his computer
Then I woke up in my bed
With a cherry on my head.

Jonty Fox (10)
William De Yaxley CE Academy, Yaxley

Koala

K ing of the trees
O ne of the fiercest animals you can meet
A ny animal you will meet, the koala is the most sweet
L azy, lovable and lovely
A ll of the above, the koala is all I love.

Ellie Renno (9)
William De Yaxley CE Academy, Yaxley

Dreaming Of My Holiday

H ere I am, asleep,
O n my holiday, in Crete.
L ying on my side,
I dream of being outside.
D are to open my eyes
A nd see blue skies.
Y es, I am happy!

Leah Moore (10)
William De Yaxley CE Academy, Yaxley

The Poem Of Life

In life, you never get what you want sometimes.
Life can be stressful or easy.
In life, if you try, you can achieve nearly anything.
In life, if you knew everything, you wouldn't have
anything to learn.

Logan Peeling (9)
William De Yaxley CE Academy, Yaxley

A Lorry Driving Through Cities

As far as I go I won't care
Through narrow roads we all are rare
Too much traffic makes me frown
Which will make me pull around
If I crash
I lose my cash
So I can't crash again.

Roy Hill (10)
William De Yaxley CE Academy, Yaxley

Gorilla In The Garden

There's a gorilla in the garden,
What is he doing here?
He's big and fluffy.

I approach him slowly, I am scared!
He looks around and smiles.
He beats his chest loudly.

Finley Templeton (10)
William De Yaxley CE Academy, Yaxley

Football

Running up and down the pitch,
Now it is time to switch.
Got to play the ball,
Pass between us all.
Shoot to score,
Hear the crowd roar.
Four nil up,
We have won the cup.

Aimee Dayman (11)
William De Yaxley CE Academy, Yaxley

Running

Running is really fun for me
It always calms me down
I really enjoy running a lot
Running is not only fun
It's also good exercise
It makes you more confident with racing.

Freya Gray (7)
William De Yaxley CE Academy, Yaxley

Once Upon A Dream

Sky is blue
Grass is green
My life is like a dream
I dream about sweets
Every day and every night
Sky is blue
Grass is green
My dream becomes real.

Teja Gintauskaite (7)
William De Yaxley CE Academy, Yaxley

Football Dream

My dream started on a football pitch,
Cristiano Ronaldo and myself,
It was hot in Portugal,
I played a football game,
I scored...
Zoom!

Theo Barton (8)
William De Yaxley CE Academy, Yaxley

Rainbow Crocodile

One day at the zoo,
I saw a rainbow crocodile,
Dancing to a tune.
It made me happy,
And I started dancing too.

Leo Cardinal (10)
William De Yaxley CE Academy, Yaxley

YoungWriters®
— Est. 1991 —

YOUNG WRITERS INFORMATION

We hope you have enjoyed reading this book – and that you will continue to in the coming years.

If you're a young writer who enjoys reading and creative writing, or the parent of an enthusiastic poet or story writer, do visit our website **www.youngwriters.co.uk**. Here you will find free competitions, workshops and games, as well as recommended reads, a poetry glossary and our blog.

If you would like to order further copies of this book, or any of our other titles, then please give us a call or visit **www.youngwriters.co.uk**.

Young Writers
Remus House
Coltsfoot Drive
Peterborough
PE2 9BF
(01733) 890066
info@youngwriters.co.uk

YoungWritersUK   **YoungWritersCW**
youngwriterscw   **youngwriterscw**